Can you make a sandcastle?

You have to get lots of wet sand.

Make a big hill of wet sand.

Dig a big moat in the sand.

Get water in a bucket. Fill the moat with the water.

Get wet sand in a bucket. Fill the bucket to the top.

Tip the bucket of wet sand on top of the hill.

It is fun to make a sandcastle.